TODAY

DATE: __/__/____

**PROJECT
SCHEDULE**

TOP THINGS TO WORK ON

_____   _____

_____   _____

_____   _____

_____   _____

PROJECT NAME/S

TARGET DEADLINE

REQUIREMENTS

OTHER TASKS

OVERVIEW OF THE PROJECT

_____

_____

_____

TODAY

DATE: __/__/____

TOP THINGS TO WORK ON

PROJECT NAME/S

TARGET DEADLINE

REQUIREMENTS

OTHER TASKS

OVERVIEW OF THE PROJECT

TODAY

DATE: __/__/____

TOP THINGS TO WORK ON

_____   _____

_____   _____

_____   _____

_____   _____

PROJECT NAME/S

TARGET DEADLINE

REQUIREMENTS

OTHER TASKS

OVERVIEW OF THE PROJECT

_____

_____

_____

TODAY

DATE: __/__/____

TOP THINGS TO WORK ON

PROJECT NAME/S

TARGET DEADLINE

REQUIREMENTS

OTHER TASKS

OVERVIEW OF THE PROJECT

TODAY

DATE: __/__/____

TOP THINGS TO WORK ON

PROJECT NAME/S

TARGET DEADLINE

REQUIREMENTS

OTHER TASKS

OVERVIEW OF THE PROJECT

TODAY

DATE: __/__/____

TOP THINGS TO WORK ON

_____   _____

_____   _____

_____   _____

_____   _____

PROJECT NAME/S

TARGET DEADLINE

REQUIREMENTS

OTHER TASKS

OVERVIEW OF THE PROJECT

_____

_____

_____

TODAY

DATE: __/__/____

TOP THINGS TO WORK ON

_____   _____

_____   _____

_____   _____

_____   _____

PROJECT NAME/S

TARGET DEADLINE

REQUIREMENTS

OTHER TASKS

OVERVIEW OF THE PROJECT

_____

_____

_____

TODAY

DATE: __/__/____

TOP THINGS TO WORK ON

PROJECT NAME/S

TARGET DEADLINE

REQUIREMENTS

OTHER TASKS

OVERVIEW OF THE PROJECT

TODAY

DATE: __/__/____

TOP THINGS TO WORK ON

_____   _____

_____   _____

_____   _____

_____   _____

PROJECT NAME/S

TARGET DEADLINE

REQUIREMENTS

OTHER TASKS

OVERVIEW OF THE PROJECT

_____

_____

_____

TODAY

DATE: __/__/____

TOP THINGS TO WORK ON

_____	_____
_____	_____
_____	_____
_____	_____

PROJECT NAME/S

TARGET DEADLINE

REQUIREMENTS

OTHER TASKS

OVERVIEW OF THE PROJECT

_____

_____

_____

TODAY

DATE: __/__/____

TOP THINGS TO WORK ON

_____ _____

_____ _____

_____ _____

_____ _____

PROJECT NAME/S

TARGET DEADLINE

REQUIREMENTS

OTHER TASKS

OVERVIEW OF THE PROJECT

_____

_____

_____

TODAY

DATE: __/__/____

TOP THINGS TO WORK ON

_____   _____

_____   _____

_____   _____

_____   _____

PROJECT NAME/S

TARGET DEADLINE

REQUIREMENTS

OTHER TASKS

OVERVIEW OF THE PROJECT

_____

_____

_____

TODAY

DATE: __/__/____

PROJECT
SCHEDULE

TOP THINGS TO WORK ON

_____   _____

_____   _____

_____   _____

_____   _____

PROJECT NAME/S

TARGET DEADLINE

REQUIREMENTS

OTHER TASKS

OVERVIEW OF THE PROJECT

_____

_____

_____

TODAY

DATE: __/__/____

TOP THINGS TO WORK ON

PROJECT NAME/S

TARGET DEADLINE

REQUIREMENTS

OTHER TASKS

OVERVIEW OF THE PROJECT

TODAY

DATE: __/__/____

TOP THINGS TO WORK ON

_____	_____
_____	_____
_____	_____
_____	_____

PROJECT NAME/S

TARGET DEADLINE

REQUIREMENTS

OTHER TASKS

OVERVIEW OF THE PROJECT

_____
_____
_____

TODAY

DATE: __/__/____

TOP THINGS TO WORK ON

_____   _____

_____   _____

_____   _____

_____   _____

PROJECT NAME/S

TARGET DEADLINE

REQUIREMENTS

OTHER TASKS

OVERVIEW OF THE PROJECT

_____

_____

_____

TODAY

DATE: __/__/____

TOP THINGS TO WORK ON

_____   _____

_____   _____

_____   _____

_____   _____

PROJECT NAME/S

TARGET DEADLINE

REQUIREMENTS

OTHER TASKS

OVERVIEW OF THE PROJECT

_____

_____

_____

TODAY

DATE: __/__/____

TOP THINGS TO WORK ON

PROJECT NAME/S

TARGET DEADLINE

REQUIREMENTS

OTHER TASKS

OVERVIEW OF THE PROJECT

TODAY

DATE: __/__/____

TOP THINGS TO WORK ON

PROJECT NAME/S

TARGET DEADLINE

REQUIREMENTS

OTHER TASKS

OVERVIEW OF THE PROJECT

TODAY

DATE: __/__/____

TOP THINGS TO WORK ON

PROJECT NAME/S

TARGET DEADLINE

REQUIREMENTS

OTHER TASKS

OVERVIEW OF THE PROJECT

TODAY

DATE: __/__/____

TOP THINGS TO WORK ON

_____   _____

_____   _____

_____   _____

_____   _____

PROJECT NAME/S

TARGET DEADLINE

REQUIREMENTS

OTHER TASKS

OVERVIEW OF THF PROJECT

_____

_____

_____

TODAY

DATE: __/__/____

TOP THINGS TO WORK ON

PROJECT NAME/S

TARGET DEADLINE

REQUIREMENTS

OTHER TASKS

OVERVIEW OF THE PROJECT

TODAY

DATE: __/__/____

TOP THINGS TO WORK ON

_____   _____

_____   _____

_____   _____

_____   _____

PROJECT NAME/S

TARGET DEADLINE

REQUIREMENTS

OTHER TASKS

OVERVIEW OF THE PROJECT

_____

_____

_____

TODAY

DATE: __/__/____

TOP THINGS TO WORK ON

_____   _____

_____   _____

_____   _____

_____   _____

PROJECT NAME/S

TARGET DEADLINE

REQUIREMENTS

OTHER TASKS

OVERVIEW OF THE PROJECT

_____

_____

_____

TODAY

DATE: __/__/____

TOP THINGS TO WORK ON

PROJECT NAME/S

TARGET DEADLINE

REQUIREMENTS

OTHER TASKS

OVERVIEW OF THE PROJECT

TODAY

DATE: __/__/____

TOP THINGS TO WORK ON

_____	_____
_____	_____
_____	_____
_____	_____

PROJECT NAME/S

TARGET DEADLINE

REQUIREMENTS

OTHER TASKS

OVERVIEW OF THE PROJECT

_____

_____

_____

TODAY

DATE: __/__/____

TOP THINGS TO WORK ON

PROJECT NAME/S

TARGET DEADLINE

REQUIREMENTS

OTHER TASKS

OVERVIEW OF THE PROJECT

TODAY

DATE: __/__/____

TOP THINGS TO WORK ON

_____   _____
_____   _____
_____   _____
_____   _____

PROJECT NAME/S

TARGET DEADLINE

REQUIREMENTS

OTHER TASKS

OVERVIEW OF THE PROJECT

_____
_____
_____

TODAY

DATE: __/__/____

TOP THINGS TO WORK ON

PROJECT NAME/S

TARGET DEADLINE

REQUIREMENTS

OTHER TASKS

OVERVIEW OF THE PROJECT

TODAY

DATE: __/__/____

TOP THINGS TO WORK ON

PROJECT NAME/S

TARGET DEADLINE

REQUIREMENTS

OTHER TASKS

OVERVIEW OF THE PROJECT

TODAY

DATE: __/__/____

TOP THINGS TO WORK ON

_____   _____

_____   _____

_____   _____

_____   _____

PROJECT NAME/S

TARGET DEADLINE

REQUIREMENTS

OTHER TASKS

OVERVIEW OF THE PROJECT

_____

_____

_____

TODAY

DATE: __/__/____

TOP THINGS TO WORK ON

_____   _____

_____   _____

_____   _____

_____   _____

PROJECT NAME/S

TARGET DEADLINE

REQUIREMENTS

OTHER TASKS

OVERVIEW OF THE PROJECT

_____

_____

_____

TODAY

DATE: __/__/____

TOP THINGS TO WORK ON

PROJECT NAME/S

TARGET DEADLINE

REQUIREMENTS

OTHER TASKS

OVERVIEW OF THE PROJECT

TODAY

DATE: __/__/____

PROJECT
SCHEDULE

TOP THINGS TO WORK ON

PROJECT NAME/S

TARGET DEADLINE

REQUIREMENTS

OTHER TASKS

OVERVIEW OF THE PROJECT

TODAY

DATE: __/__/____

TOP THINGS TO WORK ON

PROJECT NAME/S

TARGET DEADLINE

REQUIREMENTS

OTHER TASKS

OVERVIEW OF THE PROJECT

TODAY

DATE: __/__/____

TOP THINGS TO WORK ON

PROJECT NAME/S

TARGET DEADLINE

REQUIREMENTS

OTHER TASKS

OVERVIEW OF THE PROJECT

TODAY

DATE: __/__/____

TOP THINGS TO WORK ON

PROJECT NAME/S

TARGET DEADLINE

REQUIREMENTS

OTHER TASKS

OVERVIEW OF THE PROJECT

TODAY

DATE: __/__/____

TOP THINGS TO WORK ON

_____   _____

_____   _____

_____   _____

_____   _____

PROJECT NAME/S

TARGET DEADLINE

REQUIREMENTS

OTHER TASKS

OVERVIEW OF THE PROJECT

_____

_____

_____

TODAY

DATE: __/__/____

TOP THINGS TO WORK ON

PROJECT NAME/S

TARGET DEADLINE

REQUIREMENTS

OTHER TASKS

OVERVIEW OF THE PROJECT

TODAY

DATE: __/__/____

TOP THINGS TO WORK ON

_____   _____

_____   _____

_____   _____

_____   _____

PROJECT NAME/S

TARGET DEADLINE

REQUIREMENTS

OTHER TASKS

OVERVIEW OF THE PROJECT

_____

_____

_____

TODAY

DATE: __/__/____

TOP THINGS TO WORK ON

_____   _____
_____   _____
_____   _____
_____   _____

PROJECT NAME/S

TARGET DEADLINE

REQUIREMENTS

OTHER TASKS

OVERVIEW OF THE PROJECT

_____
_____
_____

TODAY

DATE: __/__/____

TOP THINGS TO WORK ON

_____   _____

_____   _____

_____   _____

_____   _____

PROJECT NAME/S

TARGET DEADLINE

REQUIREMENTS

OTHER TASKS

OVERVIEW OF THE PROJECT

_____

_____

_____

TODAY

DATE: __/__/____

TOP THINGS TO WORK ON

_____   _____

_____   _____

_____   _____

_____   _____

PROJECT NAME/S

TARGET DEADLINE

REQUIREMENTS

OTHER TASKS

OVERVIEW OF THE PROJECT

_____

_____

_____

TODAY

DATE: __/__/____

TOP THINGS TO WORK ON

_____   _____

_____   _____

_____   _____

_____   _____

PROJECT NAME/S

TARGET DEADLINE

REQUIREMENTS

OTHER TASKS

OVERVIEW OF THE PROJECT

_____

_____

_____

TODAY

DATE: __/__/____

TOP THINGS TO WORK ON

PROJECT NAME/S

TARGET DEADLINE

REQUIREMENTS

OTHER TASKS

OVERVIEW OF THE PROJECT

TODAY

DATE: __/__/____

TOP THINGS TO WORK ON

PROJECT NAME/S

TARGET DEADLINE

REQUIREMENTS

OTHER TASKS

OVERVIEW OF THE PROJECT

TODAY

DATE: __/__/____

TOP THINGS TO WORK ON

_____   _____

_____   _____

_____   _____

_____   _____

PROJECT NAME/S

TARGET DEADLINE

REQUIREMENTS

OTHER TASKS

OVERVIEW OF THE PROJECT

_____

_____

_____

TODAY

DATE: __/__/____

TOP THINGS TO WORK ON

_____   _____

_____   _____

_____   _____

_____   _____

PROJECT NAME/S

TARGET DEADLINE

REQUIREMENTS

OTHER TASKS

OVERVIEW OF THE PROJECT

_____

_____

_____

TODAY

DATE: __/__/____

TOP THINGS TO WORK ON

PROJECT NAME/S

TARGET DEADLINE

REQUIREMENTS

OTHER TASKS

OVERVIEW OF THE PROJECT

TODAY

DATE: __/__/____

TOP THINGS TO WORK ON

PROJECT NAME/S

TARGET DEADLINE

REQUIREMENTS

OTHER TASKS

OVERVIEW OF THE PROJECT

TODAY

DATE: __/__/____

TOP THINGS TO WORK ON

_____   _____

_____   _____

_____   _____

_____   _____

PROJECT NAME/S

TARGET DEADLINE

REQUIREMENTS

OTHER TASKS

OVERVIEW OF THE PROJECT

_____

_____

_____

TODAY

DATE: __/__/____

TOP THINGS TO WORK ON

_____ _____

_____ _____

_____ _____

_____ _____

PROJECT NAME/S

TARGET DEADLINE

REQUIREMENTS

OTHER TASKS

OVERVIEW OF THE PROJECT

_____

_____

_____

TODAY

DATE: __/__/____

TOP THINGS TO WORK ON

PROJECT NAME/S

TARGET DEADLINE

REQUIREMENTS

OTHER TASKS

OVERVIEW OF THE PROJECT

TODAY

DATE: __/__/____

TOP THINGS TO WORK ON

_____   _____

_____   _____

_____   _____

_____   _____

PROJECT NAME/S

TARGET DEADLINE

REQUIREMENTS

OTHER TASKS

OVERVIEW OF THE PROJECT

_____

_____

_____

TODAY

DATE: __/__/____

TOP THINGS TO WORK ON

_____   _____

_____   _____

_____   _____

_____   _____

PROJECT NAME/S

TARGET DEADLINE

REQUIREMENTS

OTHER TASKS

OVERVIEW OF THE PROJECT

_____

_____

_____

TODAY

DATE: __/__/____

TOP THINGS TO WORK ON

PROJECT NAME/S

TARGET DEADLINE

REQUIREMENTS

OTHER TASKS

OVERVIEW OF THE PROJECT

TODAY

DATE: __/__/____

TOP THINGS TO WORK ON

_____   _____
_____   _____
_____   _____
_____   _____

PROJECT NAME/S

TARGET DEADLINE

REQUIREMENTS

OTHER TASKS

OVERVIEW OF THE PROJECT

_____
_____
_____

TODAY

DATE: __/__/____

TOP THINGS TO WORK ON

_____   _____

_____   _____

_____   _____

_____   _____

PROJECT NAME/S

TARGET DEADLINE

REQUIREMENTS

OTHER TASKS

OVERVIEW OF THE PROJECT

_____

_____

_____

TODAY

DATE: __/__/____

TOP THINGS TO WORK ON

_____   _____
_____   _____
_____   _____
_____   _____

PROJECT NAME/S

TARGET DEADLINE

REQUIREMENTS

OTHER TASKS

OVERVIEW OF THE PROJECT

_____
_____
_____

TODAY

DATE: __/__/____

TOP THINGS TO WORK ON

_____   _____

_____   _____

_____   _____

_____   _____

PROJECT NAME/S

TARGET DEADLINE

REQUIREMENTS

OTHER TASKS

OVERVIEW OF THE PROJECT

_____

_____

_____

TODAY

DATE: __/__/____

TOP THINGS TO WORK ON

_____   _____

_____   _____

_____   _____

_____   _____

PROJECT NAME/S

TARGET DEADLINE

REQUIREMENTS

OTHER TASKS

OVERVIEW OF THE PROJECT

_____

_____

_____

TODAY

DATE: __/__/____

TOP THINGS TO WORK ON

_____   _____

_____   _____

_____   _____

_____   _____

PROJECT NAME/S

TARGET DEADLINE

REQUIREMENTS

OTHER TASKS

OVERVIEW OF THE PROJECT

_____

_____

_____

TODAY

DATE: __/__/____

TOP THINGS TO WORK ON

_____   _____

_____   _____

_____   _____

_____   _____

PROJECT NAME/S

TARGET DEADLINE

REQUIREMENTS

OTHER TASKS

OVERVIEW OF THE PROJECT

_____

_____

_____

TODAY

DATE: __/__/____

TOP THINGS TO WORK ON

PROJECT NAME/S

TARGET DEADLINE

REQUIREMENTS

OTHER TASKS

OVERVIEW OF THE PROJECT

TODAY

DATE: __/__/____

TOP THINGS TO WORK ON

PROJECT NAME/S

TARGET DEADLINE

REQUIREMENTS

OTHER TASKS

OVERVIEW OF THE PROJECT

TODAY

DATE: __/__/____

TOP THINGS TO WORK ON

_____   _____

_____   _____

_____   _____

_____   _____

PROJECT NAME/S

TARGET DEADLINE

REQUIREMENTS

OTHER TASKS

OVERVIEW OF THE PROJECT

_____

_____

_____

TODAY

DATE: __/__/____

TOP THINGS TO WORK ON

_____   _____

_____   _____

_____   _____

_____   _____

PROJECT NAME/S

TARGET DEADLINE

REQUIREMENTS

OTHER TASKS

OVERVIEW OF THE PROJECT

_____

_____

_____

TODAY

DATE: __/__/____

TOP THINGS TO WORK ON

_____   _____
_____   _____
_____   _____
_____   _____

PROJECT NAME/S

TARGET DEADLINE

REQUIREMENTS

OTHER TASKS

OVERVIEW OF THE PROJECT

_____
_____
_____

TODAY

DATE: __/__/____

TOP THINGS TO WORK ON

PROJECT NAME/S

TARGET DEADLINE

REQUIREMENTS

OTHER TASKS

OVERVIEW OF THE PROJECT

TODAY

DATE: __/__/____

TOP THINGS TO WORK ON

_____   _____

_____   _____

_____   _____

_____   _____

PROJECT NAME/S

TARGET DEADLINE

REQUIREMENTS

OTHER TASKS

OVERVIEW OF THE PROJECT

_____

_____

_____

TODAY

DATE: __/__/____

TOP THINGS TO WORK ON

_____   _____
_____   _____
_____   _____
_____   _____

PROJECT NAME/S

TARGET DEADLINE

REQUIREMENTS

OTHER TASKS

OVERVIEW OF THE PROJECT

_____
_____
_____

TODAY

DATE: __/__/____

TOP THINGS TO WORK ON

_____   _____

_____   _____

_____   _____

_____   _____

PROJECT NAME/S

TARGET DEADLINE

REQUIREMENTS

OTHER TASKS

OVERVIEW OF THE PROJECT

_____

_____

_____

TODAY

DATE: __/__/____

TOP THINGS TO WORK ON

_____   _____

_____   _____

_____   _____

_____   _____

PROJECT NAME/S

TARGET DEADLINE

REQUIREMENTS

OTHER TASKS

OVERVIEW OF THE PROJECT

_____

_____

_____

TODAY

DATE: __/__/____

TOP THINGS TO WORK ON

_____   _____

_____   _____

_____   _____

_____   _____

PROJECT NAME/S

TARGET DEADLINE

REQUIREMENTS

OTHER TASKS

OVERVIEW OF THE PROJECT

_____

_____

_____

TODAY

DATE: __/__/____

TOP THINGS TO WORK ON

_____   _____
_____   _____
_____   _____
_____   _____

PROJECT NAME/S

TARGET DEADLINE

REQUIREMENTS

OTHER TASKS

OVERVIEW OF THE PROJECT

_____
_____
_____

TODAY

DATE: __/__/____

TOP THINGS TO WORK ON

PROJECT NAME/S

TARGET DEADLINE

REQUIREMENTS

OTHER TASKS

OVERVIEW OF THE PROJECT

TODAY

DATE: __/__/____

TOP THINGS TO WORK ON

_____   _____

_____   _____

_____   _____

_____   _____

PROJECT NAME/S

TARGET DEADLINE

REQUIREMENTS

OTHER TASKS

OVERVIEW OF THE PROJECT

_____

_____

_____

TODAY

DATE: __/__/____

TOP THINGS TO WORK ON

_____   _____
_____   _____
_____   _____
_____   _____

PROJECT NAME/S

TARGET DEADLINE

REQUIREMENTS

OTHER TASKS

OVERVIEW OF THE PROJECT

_____
_____
_____

TODAY

DATE: __/__/____

TOP THINGS TO WORK ON

_____   _____

_____   _____

_____   _____

_____   _____

PROJECT NAME/S

TARGET DEADLINE

REQUIREMENTS

OTHER TASKS

OVERVIEW OF THE PROJECT

_____

_____

_____

TODAY

DATE: __/__/____

TOP THINGS TO WORK ON

_____   _____

_____   _____

_____   _____

_____   _____

PROJECT NAME/S

TARGET DEADLINE

REQUIREMENTS

OTHER TASKS

OVERVIEW OF THE PROJECT

_____

_____

_____

TODAY

DATE: __/__/____

TOP THINGS TO WORK ON

PROJECT NAME/S

TARGET DEADLINE

REQUIREMENTS

OTHER TASKS

OVERVIEW OF THE PROJECT

TODAY

DATE: __/__/____

TOP THINGS TO WORK ON

_____   _____

_____   _____

_____   _____

_____   _____

PROJECT NAME/S

TARGET DEADLINE

REQUIREMENTS

OTHER TASKS

OVERVIEW OF THE PROJECT

_____

_____

_____

TODAY

DATE: __/__/____

TOP THINGS TO WORK ON

_____	_____
_____	_____
_____	_____
_____	_____

PROJECT NAME/S

TARGET DEADLINE

REQUIREMENTS

OTHER TASKS

OVERVIEW OF THE PROJECT

_____

_____

_____

TODAY

DATE: __/__/____

TOP THINGS TO WORK ON

_____	_____
_____	_____
_____	_____
_____	_____

PROJECT NAME/S

TARGET DEADLINE

REQUIREMENTS

OTHER TASKS

OVERVIEW OF THE PROJECT

_____

_____

_____

TODAY

DATE: __/__/____

TOP THINGS TO WORK ON

_____ _____

_____ _____

_____ _____

_____ _____

PROJECT NAME/S

TARGET DEADLINE

REQUIREMENTS

OTHER TASKS

OVERVIEW OF THE PROJECT

_____

_____

_____

TODAY

DATE: __/__/____

TOP THINGS TO WORK ON

_____   _____

_____   _____

_____   _____

_____   _____

PROJECT NAME/S

TARGET DEADLINE

REQUIREMENTS

OTHER TASKS

OVERVIEW OF THE PROJECT

_____

_____

_____

TODAY

DATE: __/__/____

TOP THINGS TO WORK ON

_____   _____

_____   _____

_____   _____

_____   _____

PROJECT NAME/S

TARGET DEADLINE

REQUIREMENTS

OTHER TASKS

OVERVIEW OF THE PROJECT

_____

_____

_____

TODAY

DATE: __/__/____

TOP THINGS TO WORK ON

PROJECT NAME/S

TARGET DEADLINE

REQUIREMENTS

OTHER TASKS

OVERVIEW OF THE PROJECT

TODAY

DATE: __/__/____

TOP THINGS TO WORK ON

_____   _____

_____   _____

_____   _____

_____   _____

PROJECT NAME/S

TARGET DEADLINE

REQUIREMENTS

OTHER TASKS

OVERVIEW OF THE PROJECT

_____

_____

_____

TODAY

DATE: __/__/____

TOP THINGS TO WORK ON

_____   _____
_____   _____
_____   _____
_____   _____

PROJECT NAME/S

TARGET DEADLINE

REQUIREMENTS

OTHER TASKS

OVERVIEW OF THE PROJECT

_____
_____
_____

TODAY

DATE: __/__/____

TOP THINGS TO WORK ON

PROJECT NAME/S

TARGET DEADLINE

REQUIREMENTS

OTHER TASKS

OVERVIEW OF THE PROJECT

TODAY

DATE: __/__/____

TOP THINGS TO WORK ON

_____	_____
_____	_____
_____	_____
_____	_____

PROJECT NAME/S

TARGET DEADLINE

REQUIREMENTS

OTHER TASKS

OVERVIEW OF THE PROJECT

_____

_____

_____

TODAY

DATE: __/__/____

TOP THINGS TO WORK ON

_____   _____

_____   _____

_____   _____

_____   _____

PROJECT NAME/S

TARGET DEADLINE

REQUIREMENTS

OTHER TASKS

OVERVIEW OF THE PROJECT

_____

_____

_____

TODAY

DATE: __/__/____

TOP THINGS TO WORK ON

_____   _____
_____   _____
_____   _____
_____   _____

PROJECT NAME/S

TARGET DEADLINE

REQUIREMENTS

OTHER TASKS

OVERVIEW OF THE PROJECT

_____
_____
_____

TODAY

DATE: __/__/____

TOP THINGS TO WORK ON

_____ _____

_____ _____

_____ _____

_____ _____

PROJECT NAME/S

TARGET DEADLINE

REQUIREMENTS

OTHER TASKS

OVERVIEW OF THE PROJECT

_____

_____

_____

TODAY

DATE: __/__/____

TOP THINGS TO WORK ON

PROJECT NAME/S

TARGET DEADLINE

REQUIREMENTS

OTHER TASKS

OVERVIEW OF THE PROJECT

TODAY

DATE: __/__/____

TOP THINGS TO WORK ON

_____   _____
_____   _____
_____   _____
_____   _____

PROJECT NAME/S

TARGET DEADLINE

REQUIREMENTS

OTHER TASKS

OVERVIEW OF THE PROJECT

_____
_____
_____

TODAY

DATE: __/__/____

TOP THINGS TO WORK ON

PROJECT NAME/S

TARGET DEADLINE

REQUIREMENTS

OTHER TASKS

OVERVIEW OF THE PROJECT

TODAY

DATE: __/__/____

TOP THINGS TO WORK ON

_____   _____

_____   _____

_____   _____

_____   _____

PROJECT NAME/S

TARGET DEADLINE

REQUIREMENTS

OTHER TASKS

OVERVIEW OF THE PROJECT

_____

_____

_____

TODAY

DATE: __/__/____

TOP THINGS TO WORK ON

_____   _____

_____   _____

_____   _____

_____   _____

PROJECT NAME/S

TARGET DEADLINE

REQUIREMENTS

OTHER TASKS

OVERVIEW OF THE PROJECT

_____

_____

_____

TODAY

DATE: __/__/____

TOP THINGS TO WORK ON

_____   _____

_____   _____

_____   _____

_____   _____

PROJECT NAME/S

TARGET DEADLINE

REQUIREMENTS

OTHER TASKS

OVERVIEW OF THE PROJECT

_____

_____

_____

TODAY

DATE: __/__/____

TOP THINGS TO WORK ON

_____   _____

_____   _____

_____   _____

_____   _____

PROJECT NAME/S

TARGET DEADLINE

REQUIREMENTS

OTHER TASKS

OVERVIEW OF THE PROJECT

_____

_____

_____

TODAY

DATE: __/__/____

TOP THINGS TO WORK ON

_____   _____

_____   _____

_____   _____

_____   _____

PROJECT NAME/S

TARGET DEADLINE

REQUIREMENTS

OTHER TASKS

OVERVIEW OF THE PROJECT

_____

_____

_____

TODAY

DATE: __/__/____

TOP THINGS TO WORK ON

_____   _____
_____   _____
_____   _____
_____   _____

PROJECT NAME/S

TARGET DEADLINE

REQUIREMENTS

OTHER TASKS

OVERVIEW OF THE PROJECT

_____
_____
_____

TODAY

DATE: __/__/____

TOP THINGS TO WORK ON

_____   _____

_____   _____

_____   _____

_____   _____

PROJECT NAME/S

TARGET DEADLINE

REQUIREMENTS

OTHER TASKS

OVERVIEW OF THE PROJECT

_____

_____

_____

TODAY

DATE: __/__/____

TOP THINGS TO WORK ON

PROJECT NAME/S

TARGET DEADLINE

REQUIREMENTS

OTHER TASKS

OVERVIEW OF THE PROJECT

TODAY

DATE: __/__/____

TOP THINGS TO WORK ON

_____   _____

_____   _____

_____   _____

_____   _____

PROJECT NAME/S

TARGET DEADLINE

REQUIREMENTS

OTHER TASKS

OVERVIEW OF THE PROJECT

_____

_____

_____

TODAY

DATE: __/__/____

TOP THINGS TO WORK ON

_____   _____

_____   _____

_____   _____

_____   _____

PROJECT NAME/S

TARGET DEADLINE

REQUIREMENTS

OTHER TASKS

OVERVIEW OF THE PROJECT

_____

_____

_____

TODAY

DATE: __/__/____

TOP THINGS TO WORK ON

_____	_____
_____	_____
_____	_____
_____	_____

PROJECT NAME/S

TARGET DEADLINE

REQUIREMENTS

OTHER TASKS

OVERVIEW OF THE PROJECT

_____

_____

_____

TODAY

DATE: __/__/____

TOP THINGS TO WORK ON

_____   _____

_____   _____

_____   _____

_____   _____

PROJECT NAME/S

TARGET DEADLINE

REQUIREMENTS

OTHER TASKS

OVERVIEW OF THE PROJECT

_____

_____

_____

TODAY

DATE: __/__/____

TOP THINGS TO WORK ON

PROJECT NAME/S

TARGET DEADLINE

REQUIREMENTS

OTHER TASKS

OVERVIEW OF THE PROJECT

TODAY

DATE: __/__/____

TOP THINGS TO WORK ON

_____   _____
_____   _____
_____   _____
_____   _____

PROJECT NAME/S

TARGET DEADLINE

REQUIREMENTS

OTHER TASKS

OVERVIEW OF THE PROJECT

_____
_____
_____

TODAY

DATE: __/__/____

TOP THINGS TO WORK ON

PROJECT NAME/S

TARGET DEADLINE

REQUIREMENTS

OTHER TASKS

OVERVIEW OF THE PROJECT

TODAY

DATE: __/__/____

TOP THINGS TO WORK ON

_____   _____

_____   _____

_____   _____

_____   _____

PROJECT NAME/S

TARGET DEADLINE

REQUIREMENTS

OTHER TASKS

OVERVIEW OF THE PROJECT

_____

_____

_____

TODAY

DATE: __/__/____

TOP THINGS TO WORK ON

_____   _____

_____   _____

_____   _____

_____   _____

PROJECT NAME/S

TARGET DEADLINE

REQUIREMENTS

OTHER TASKS

OVERVIEW OF THE PROJECT

_____

_____

_____

TODAY

DATE: __/__/____

TOP THINGS TO WORK ON

PROJECT NAME/S

TARGET DEADLINE

REQUIREMENTS

OTHER TASKS

OVERVIEW OF THE PROJECT

TODAY

DATE: __/__/____

TOP THINGS TO WORK ON

PROJECT NAME/S

TARGET DEADLINE

REQUIREMENTS

OTHER TASKS

OVERVIEW OF THE PROJECT

TODAY

DATE: __/__/____

TOP THINGS TO WORK ON

_____	_____
_____	_____
_____	_____
_____	_____

PROJECT NAME/S

TARGET DEADLINE

REQUIREMENTS

OTHER TASKS

OVERVIEW OF THE PROJECT

_____

_____

_____

TODAY

DATE: __/__/____

TOP THINGS TO WORK ON

_____   _____

_____   _____

_____   _____

_____   _____

PROJECT NAME/S

TARGET DEADLINE

REQUIREMENTS

OTHER TASKS

OVERVIEW OF THE PROJECT

_____

_____

_____

TODAY

DATE: __/__/____

TOP THINGS TO WORK ON

PROJECT NAME/S

TARGET DEADLINE

REQUIREMENTS

OTHER TASKS

OVERVIEW OF THE PROJECT